How To Be a Successful Business Weed

A new look at how plants mirror
successful management

Mike Pearce

DEDICATION

This book is dedicated to all plant lovers and botany
lecturers as well as to Samuel Pearce (Cinematographer)
and all those young self-employed people trying to make
their way in the business world.

CONTENTS

CONTENTS CONTINUED

Introduction

Follow the plants, a must to read, here is a new approach to business ideas through gardeners' secrets.

Plants have been around a long time. They have withstood many major changes over the earth's surface including those caused by man. This book links their structure, behaviour and resolution to succeed with that seen in types of management systems. It also opens up a panorama for those who know little about plants and gardening.

"Don't judge each day by the harvest you reap but by the seeds that you plant'.

Robert Louis Stevenson

1 SEEDS

*'It is like a mustard seed,
which a man took and cast into
his garden and it grew, and
waxed a great tree; and the
fowls of the air lodged in the
branches of it.'*

Bible (King James Version) Luke 13:19

Seeds are the most important investment for a business. They only need to be small to grow big.

- **PLANT THE SEEDS OF YOUR BUSINESS IN THE RIGHT PLACE.**

- **PLANT THEM AT THE RIGHT TIME.**

- **MAKE SURE SEEDS HAVE AN INITIAL ENERGY STORE E.G. FINANCIAL SUPPORT) TO START OFF GROWTH.**

- **ENSURE SEEDS HAVE A PROTECTIVE OUTER LAYER TO STOP NEGATIVE INFLUENCES AND MECHANICAL INJURIES.**

- **LOOK OUT FOR COMPETITORS IN SAME AREA.**

2 CHOICE

'It's our choices, Harry, that shows what we truly are, far more than our abilities.'

Harry Potter Chamber of Secrets

J.K. Rowling (2002)

There is a huge selection of seeds you can plant and it is important to get this right at the start

- **ENSURE SEEDS ARE OF GOOD QUALITY.**

- **ENSURE SEEDS ARE RESISTANT AND CORRECT VARIETY.**

- **MAKE SURE DIFFERENT REQUIREMENTS ARE MET.**

- **ENSURE FINAL PRODUCT FITS EXACTLY WHAT IT IS INTENDED TO BE.**

3 VIABILITY

'The creation of a thousand forests is in one acorn'

Ralph Waldo Emerson. Essay, History, (1841)

Flowering plants have worked with nature to get the size and shape of the seed right to be successful but still some seeds will not be viable and only a proportion will germinate and this must be expected.

- **ENSURE SEEDS ARE IN THE RIGHT CONDITIONS AND MONITOR PROGRESS AT THE START.**

- **SMALL SEEDS NEED LESS COVER.**

- **MAY NEED TO REMOVE AN INITIAL COVERING /BARRIER FOR GERMINATION.**

- **PICK OUT, TO PREVENT OVER CROWDING WHEN BUSINESS STARTS TO GERMINATE AND GROW.**

- **PLAN A SCHEDULE FOR INITIAL GROWTH AND HOW EXTENSIVE YOU WANT TO SPREAD WITH POSSIBLE METHODS OF CONTROL.**

- **LOOK AT NEW KINDS OF TECHNOLOGY TO SUPPORT YOUR EVOLVING SYSTEMS.**

- **GET EVERYBODY TO BE COMMITTED TO QUALITY AT EVERY STAGE OF DEVELOPMENT.**

- **QUALITY IS THE DEGREE OF EXCELLENCE AND IS EXPECTED WHEN A PRODUCT IS RELEASED.**

- **DURABILITY IS ESSENTIAL.**

4 HABITAT

'Every cock will crow upon his own dunghill.'

Proverb mid-13th Century from Adagio of Erasmus

Each area of development can be considered as a staff member's habitat where they effect with others and the system. Customers must be respected and in-house projects developed to move things forward.

- **MANAGEMENT MUST DETERMINE THE CLIMATE BOTH LOCAL AND TOTAL.**

- **BEST TO LOOK AT LOCAL EFFECTS FIRST.**

- **BEWARE OF MICROCLIMATES THAT COULD IMPOSE LIMITATIONS.**

- EACH EMPLOYEE IS LIKE A PIECE IN A JIGSAW PUZZLE AND MANAGERS MUST FIRST FIND OUT HOW EACH FITS TOGETHER TO PRESENT THE WHOLE PICTURE.

- LOOK FOR COMPETITION. MAY NOT BE OBVIOUS BUT CAN OPERATE BY AFFECTING PHYSICAL OR EMOTIONAL STRESS.

- LONG WAITS CAN CAUSE ANXIETY AND STRESS.

- LOOK FOR EFFECTS THAT COULD BE CAUSED BY PHYSICAL, INTELLECTUAL.

- LANGUAGE PROBLEMS, EMOTIONAL OR SOCIAL ASPECTS WHICH IN TURN WILL AFFECT THE BUSINESS BALANCE.

- STAFF ARE NOT A COMMODITY AND THROUGH BETTER TRAINING AND UP-SKILLING CAN BECOME MORE COMMITTED.

- GET THE RIGHT FOCUS AND MAINTAIN HIGH CONTACT WITH CUSTOMERS.

- DEVELOP AND IMPLEMENT CHANGES THROUGH PROJECT MANAGEMENT.

- USE DIFFERENT EXPERTISE FOR PROJECTS AND DIFFERENT INPUTS BREAKDOWN STEPS AND WORK TOGETHER

- MONITOR PROJECT PROGRESS AGAINST PLANNED TARGET TIMES.

- **QUALITY WILL RELY ON PERFORMANCE AND RELIABILITY.**

- **CUSTOMERS ALWAYS LOOK TO FIND THE BEST.**

- **YOUR CUSTOMERS HAVE TOLERANCE LIMITS AND QUALITY HAS TO BE WEIGHED UP AGAINST COST AND USEFULNESS.**

- **NEED TO UNDERSTAND CUSTOMER NEEDS AND PROJECT FRIENDLINESS, TRUSTWORTHINESS AND GIVE ACCESS TO GOOD COMMUNICATION TO INSPIRE CONFIDENCE.**

5 STRUCTURE AND FUNCTION

'Form follows structure.'

Louis Henri Sullivan 1856-1924. The Tall Office Building. Artistically Considered, (1896)

Different types of staff and organisational structures as seen in plant tissues are important. Some may need support especially where they are establishing rhythms of growth and maturity. As with plant structure there are different roles and functions for each part

- **NOTE THAT FOR SOME PLANTING ESTABLISHMENT MAY BE SLOW.**

- **LOOK AT MAIN RESOURCES WHICH WILL TRIGGER FACILITY NEEDS.**

- IDENTIFY THE LEAST SPECIALISED AND FLEXIBLE WHO CAN CARRY OUT MOST FUNCTIONS. THESE HAVE THE ABILITY TO DIFFERENTIATE INTO OTHER ROLES UNDER SPECIAL CONDITIONS ESPECIALLY WHEN SOMETHING GOES WRONG.

- IDENTIFY THOSE WHO ARE STRONGER, MORE MATURE AND CAN FORM THE STRINGS OF THE ORGANISATION WITH A ROLE IN SUPPORT.

- IDENTIFY THOSE WHO ARE AT THEIR LEVEL AND ARE IMPORTANT STRUCTURALLY BUT MAY NOT PROGRESS FURTHER.

- IDENTIFY THOSE WHO CAN STRETCH AND PROVIDE A MEANS OF SUPPORTING THE BUSINESS BASIC NEEDS THROUGH LINKS.

- **IDENTIFY THOSE WHO FORM A SKIN AROUND THE ORGANISATION WHOSE MAIN ROLE IS PROTECTION.**

- **IDENTIFY THOSE WHO WILL FORM THE MAIN BULK OF THE ORGANISATION.**

- **INITIALLY SELECTION WILL DEPEND ON CHANCE AS WITH PUTTING OUT NEW SHOOTS AND ROOTS BUT AS ORGANISATION GROWS CERTAIN.**

- **CHARACTERISTICS AND MORE DEFINED ROLES WILL BE RECOGNISED TO BUILD UP A TEAM.**

- **NEW EMPLOYEES CAN THRIVE BUT FOR OTHERS THE HABITAT WILL BE UNFAVOURABLE AND THEY MAY LEAVE.**

- **SOME MAY REMAIN AND TOLERATE THE CONDITIONS BUT THESE CAN CHANGE OR BE MODIFIED.**

- **ENSURE COMMUNICATION IS INCREASED ACROSS ALL AREAS.**

- **MORE LAYERS OF STAFF AND MANAGEMENT CAN INCREASE COSTS FASTER THAN OUTPUT LEVELS.**

- **NEED TO LOOK FOR SIMILAR OVERLAPPING. ACTIVITIES IN DIFFERENT DEPARTMENTS WHICH COULD BE SLOWING THE FLOW AND PRODUCE BOTTLE NECKS AND REDUCE THE RANGE OF TASKS IF POSSIBLE.**

- **MAINTAIN GOOD LINKS BETWEEN SUPPLIER AND CUSTOMER WITH VISIBLE GOOD CUSTOMER SERVICE.**

6 GERMINATION

'My momma always said life was like a box of chocolates. You never know what you are going to get.'

Tom Hanks in Eric Ross 'Forrest Gump' film (1994).

Weeds often have seeds that do not need special conditions to germinate. Overspecialisation in business can become a problem in dealing with new demands put on them by the customer

- **LOOK FOR THE BEST PLACE TO GERMINATE YOUR BUSINESS.**

- **ALWAYS LOOK OUT FOR A DISASTER SOMEWHERE OR A NEW STIMULUS.**

- NOTE SOME BUSINESSES
  WILL GERMINATE FASTER
  THAN OTHERS TO GIVE
  AN EASY CROP.

- BE AWARE THAT SOME
  BUSINESSES WILL REMAIN
  HIDDEN UNDER THE
  EARTH WAITING FOR THE
  RIGHT MOMENT AND
  SOME MAY NEVER FULLY
  EMERGE SUCCESSFULLY.

- A TRIGGER MAY CAUSE
  SUCKERS TO DEVELOP ON
  THE ROOTS OF THE
  BUSINESS TO TAKE IN
  MORE SUPPLIES TO HELP
  GROWTH.

- NEED AREAS IN YOUR
  ORGANISATION WHERE
  THERE ARE SUFFICIENT
  ENERGY BUDGETS LAID
  ASIDE TO USE IN
  EXPANSION AND
  GROWTH.

7 GROWTH

'The growth of a large business is merely survival of the fittest. The American beauty rose can be produced in splendour and fragrance which bring cheer to its beholder only by sacrificing the early buds which grow up around it.'
John D Rockefeller (1839-1937)

Growth of weeds can be fast to be the first to appear in an area and overshadow any competitors. Where new opportunities are spotted in business those first at the post may have added advantage.

- **NEED TO ENSURE YOU ARE USING GOOD QUALITY STOCK AND STURDY STEMS AND ROOTS ARE DEVELOPING.**

- **DURING INITIAL GROWTH BIG AND SMALL THINGS MAY GO WRONG SO NEED TO ENSURE EXPERTS CAN TAKE ACTION IMMEDIATELY IF SOMETHING HAPPENS.**

- **IDENTIFY ANNUAL VERSUS PERENNIAL GROWTH.**

- **PROTECT AREAS OF YOUR BUSINESS NOT EXPOSED.**

- **AVOID GROWING TOO BIG TOO FAST SO AS NOT TO RUN OUT OF RESOURCES.**

- **ACCURATELY POSITION YOURSELF SO AS TO GET MAXIMUM EXPOSURE AND BE ABLE TO SPREAD AND MAKE DEEP ROOTS.**

- **REMEMBER YOU MAY REACH GREAT HEIGHTS BUT STILL NOT DOMINATE.**

- **POSITION YOURSELF LIKE YOUR PARENT COMPANY.**

- **ENSURE OFF SHOOTS HAVE THEIR OWN SUPPLIES.**

- **WHERE BRANCHES ARE EMERGING IN MANY DIRECTIONS YOU NEED TO CUT OUT AND PRUNE SIDE SHOOTS.**

- **TRAIN YOUR MAIN STEM OF BUSINESS TO ENSURE DIRECTION IS MAINTAINED. SUCCESS DEPENDS ON THE TYPES OF PATTERNS PRODUCED.**

- **YOU NEED TO BUILD UP A LOT OF PROP ROOTS AS ANCHORS BUT BEWARE OF MUD WHERE SEEDLINGS MAY BE DISLODGED BY CURRENTS.**

- BEWARE OF THOSE UNKNOWN WORKING IN THE SHADE.

- MAKE SPACE FOR UNDIFFERENTIATED ROLES THROUGHOUT THE LIFE OF THE BUSINESS WHICH MAY EVENTUALLY DIFFERENTIATE TO FORM DIFFERENT TYPES.

- NOTE THERE ARE CONSTANTS LIKE OVERALL SHAPE AND BRANCHING OUT PATTERNS, BUT YOU MAY NOT BE ABLE TO PREDICT WHERE A NEW BRANCH WILL EMERGE.

- THE CUTTING EDGE OR TIPS OF YOUR BUSINESS WILL BE WHERE A GROWTH DIRECTION CAN OCCUR. THIS IS PRIMARY GROWTH.

- **SECONDARY GROWTH INVOLVES ENLARGING PARTS OF THE ORGANISATION ALREADY FUNCTIONING. THIS MUST BE WELL DESIGNED AND ENSURE THAT EACH SECTION IS ROBUST, WITHIN THE REMIT OF THE ORGANISATION AND INCLUDES GOOD CUSTOMER AWARENESS AND COST EFFECTIVENESS.**

8 ENVIRONMENTAL CHANGES

'The parks are the lungs of London.'

Attributed to William Pitt Earl of Chatham in a speech by William Windham (1808) about encroachment of buildings on Hyde Park.

Time does not stand still an oasis can soon become a desert. It is important to monitor the flow and make preparations or start evolving new features to overcome possible changes

- **TIME SCALE AND CHANGES OVER THE YEAR ARE IMPORTANT.**

- **ENSURE YOUR WORKING ENVIRONMENT IS CLEAN AND ORDERLY AND WITHOUT WASTE BUILD UP.**

- **INFLUENTIAL FACTORS CAN BE SOCIAL ECONOMIC, EMOTIONAL, PHYSIOLOGICAL OR INTELLECTUAL AND MAY EXERT AN INFLUENCE WITH TIME OF DAY, SEASON, OR CLIMATE.**

- **YOU WILL NEVER BE ABLE TO UNDERSTAND THE TOTAL PICTURE. SMALL FACTORS MAY NOT BE KNOWN SO COMMUNICATION IS IMPORTANT.**

- **BE AWARE THAT THE INFLUENCE OF LIGHT LEVELS, TEMPERATURE, HUMIDITY AND VENTILATION CAN AFFECT THE BEHAVIOUR AND PERFORMANCE OF STAFF.**

- **THE PRESENCE OF WATER OR DRINKS DISPENSERS AND BOTTLED WATER CAN POSITIVELY CONTRIBUTE MENTALLY AND PHYSICALLY TOWARDS TASK ACHIEVEMENT.**

- **PROXIMITY OF FELLOW WORKERS, THEIR NUMBERS AND ROLES IN THE ORGANISATION CAN HAVE A BENEFICIAL OR NON BENEFICIAL EFFECT.**

- **CONSIDER LINKING (GRAFTING) NEW EMPLOYEES TO WELL EXPERIENCED ONES TO PRODUCE NEW FRUIT.**

- **DON'T WORK TOWARDS OVERCROPPING BUT USE A STAGGERED HARVEST PROCEDURE.**

- **RECOGNISE THAT SOME PEOPLE WILL BE MORE ADAPTED AND ORGANISED BEHAVIOURALLY AND HEALTHWISE THAN OTHERS LESS TOUGHENED TO THE PART.**

- **ENSURE YOU ARE AWARE OF THE FINE BALANCE THAT EXISTS WHICH MAY BE INFLUENCED BY THE SLIGHTEST CHANGE IN A SINGLE FACTOR.**

9 PARTNERSHIPS AND WORKING TOGETHER

"All for one, one for all"

The Motto of the Three Musketeers

Alexander Dumas, (1844)

To succeed partnerships are essential with the customer the supplier and between members of your own staff

- **BUSINESSES CAN BE AWOKEN AND MADE MORE INTERESTING BY INTRODUCING NEW UNCOMMON INITIATIVES WHICH GO ALONGSIDE ESTABLISHED FAVOURITES.**

- **BREAK DOWN BARRIERS BETWEEN DEPARTMENTS, POOR QUALITY IS OFTEN DUE TO A POOR SYSTEM.**

- **WHERE STAFF WORK TOGETHER THERE MAY BE A COMPLEX TANGLE OF INTERRELATIONSHIPS ALREADY FORGED SOME BEING ALLIES OTHERS NOT. SOME ONLY MANAGE TO SURVIVE DAILY WHERE DIFFICULTIES EXIST SO COMMUNICATION IS VERY IMPORTANT.**

- **NOTE AS WITH TREES, STAFF OR PRODUCTS IN ISOLATION TEND TO BE ATTACKED MORE.**

- **EACH MEMBER OF A PARTNERSHIP CAN SURVIVE ALONE BUT WORK BETTER TOGETHER.**

- **PARTNERSHIPS CAN HELP PROTECT AGAINST DISASTERS, IDENTIFY PRIORITIES AND ALLOW DIFFERENT CONTRIBUTIONS TO ACHIEVE A COMMON GOAL.**

- **STAFF NEED TO BE ABLE TO INFORM MANAGEMENT AND BE INVOLVED IN DECISIONS THROUGH QUALITY CIRCLES.THEY ALSO NEED TO BE REWARDED WITH VISIBLE ACKNOWLEDGEMENTS ETC.**

- **ALWAYS AIM TO IMPROVE CUSTOMER SERVICE AND ENHANCE PRIDE OF WORKMANSHIP THROUGH MEASURABLE OBJECTIVES.**

10 COMPETITION, DOMINANCE AND PREDATORS

'We stopped looking for monsters under our bed when we realised that they were inside us'

Charles Darwin

All people depend on other people to survive but competition will always be there and can creep in unknown like an invading fungus. Preparation for competition is essential through diversification and research. Clear understanding of costings and the elasticity of this may help reduce or even defeat competition Competition can be in different forms through cost quality delivery and flexibility

- **INCREASED COMPETITION CAN BE THROUGH TECHNOLOGY.**

- MONEY IS AN IMPORTANT MAIN DRIVER.

- LARGE BUSINESSES NEED TO PRE-EMPT COMPETITION AND NEED CAPACITY AGAINST RISKS TAKEN.

- SYSTEMS ARE NOT STATIC AND THERE ARE ALWAYS CHANGES GOING ON SO AS A MANAGER YOU NEED TO BE TOUGH AND ACCOMMODATING.

- SOME KINDS OF BUSINESS, THEIR ENVIRONMENT AND LOCALITY MAY BE SUBJECT TO HIGHER COMPETITION AND THEREFORE MORE SUSCEPTIBLE.

- **HOLES IN PARTS OF A BUSINESS CAN DISTORT RAGGED EDGES.**

- **DEEP UNDERGROUND ROOTS OF A BUSINESS CAN DEVELOP EXTENSIONS OR RUNNERS TO BREAK THROUGH THE HARDEST COMPETITION.**

- **ENSURE NO OTHER COMPANY IS FEEDING UNNOTICED ON YOUR BUSINESS.**

- **YOUR BUSINESS MUST DEVELOP DEFENCE LIKE THICK SPINES AND THICK SKIN NEARER THE OUTSIDE.**

- **ENSURE THAT TOO MUCH OVER GROWTH DOES NOT PUT YOUR HEAD OVER THE PARAPET AND INCREASE VULNERABILITY.**

- **COMPETITION MAY BE SUPERFICIAL OR DEEP ATTACK.**

- **ENSURE SMALL SOURCES OF COMPETITION ARE NOT PLACED OVER AREAS OF YOUR BUSINESS WHICH WILL HATCH OUT LATER TO DEVOUR YOUR SUCCESS.**

- **REDUCED SPACE, FLEXIBILITY AND POOR USE OF HUMAN RESOURCES CAN MAKE YOU VULNERABLE.**

- **THE GREATEST COMPETITION OCCURS WHEN A SIMILAR ORGANISATION REACHES THE SAME SIZE.**

- **DIFFERENT WAYS ARE NEEDED TO COMPETE WITH COST, QUALITY, DELIVERY OF SERVICES AND FLEXIBILITY.**

- **EXTERNAL INFLUENCES AFFECT STAFFING PROGRESS AND MOVEMENT TOWARDS FAILURE OR SUCCESS.**

- **YOU NEED TO KNOW HOW YOUR STAFF REACT UNDER CERTAIN CONDITIONS AND THEIR EXPECTATIONS.**

- **INTENSE COMPETITION BETWEEN DIFFERENT MEMBERS OF STAFF MAY BE DIFFICULT TO RECONCILE.**

- **BE AWARE THAT INDIVIDUALS ARE INFLUENCED BY THE POSITIVE OR NEGATIVE CONSEQUENCES OF THEIR ACTIONS.THIS CAN INITIATE COMPETITION.**

- **LOOK OUT FOR STRONGER CHARACTERS THAT CAN DOMINATE OTHERS WORKING BENEATH THEM. HOWEVER THE SURROUNDINGS MAY RESTRICT OR PROHIBIT THE INFLUENCE THEY HAVE.**

- **YOU NEED POSITIVE MESSAGES TO INHIBIT COMPETITION AND MAKE THE BUSINESS MORE RESISTANT.**

11 TIGHT NICHES

'I felt I was walking with destiny, and that all my past life had been but a preparation for this hour and this trial.'

Prime Minister Winston Churchill. (10th May 1940)

Small businesses may be working in a very tight niche where specialist services are provided. These can be very successful depending on demand and current trends.

- **LOOK FOR NICHES OR DEEP CRACKS IN OTHER BUSINESSES WHERE YOUR BUSINESS COULD GROW.**

- **LOOK TO COLONISING NEW TERRITORIES AND EVOLVING DIFFERENT FORMS.**

- **YOU MAY NEED TO PROTECT SMALL PARTS OF THE ORGANISATION WHICH MAY BE FRAGILE TO EXTREMES.**

- **WHERE NO PREDATORS EXIST YOU CAN EVOLVE SPECIFIC ROLES TO CATCH CUSTOM FROM UNSUSPECTING AREAS.**

- **THE MORE SPECIALISMS YOU DEVELOP THE TIGHTER METHODS THAT CAN BE USED FOR WORKER PRODUCTIVITY.**

- **PREVIOUS STAFF MAY HAVE HELPED BREAK DOWN THE SYSTEM PAVING THE WAY FOR INTRODUCING SPECIAL REQUIREMENTS.**

- **IDENTIFY PEOPLE WHO THRIVE ON MODEST CONTRIBUTIONS AND EVENTUALLY FIND A NICHE WHERE THEIR COMPETENCE CAN GROW.**

- **YOU NEED TO DEPEND ON INITIAL FRAME WORKS WHERE UNIFORMITY IS CRUCIAL TO BUILD ON.**

- **CARE HAS TO BE TAKEN TO MAKE SURE PRODUCTS ARE NOT OUT DATED. BUT TRENDS DO RE-EMERGE.**

12. AGGRESSION

'The tygers of wrath are wiser than the horses of instruction'

William Blake - The Marriage of Heaven and Hell. The Proverbs of Hell. (1790-3)

Weeds certainly show aggressive behaviour in order to dominate their surroundings. Businesses, in order to be successful, have to appear aggressive towards their competitors or they may go under.

- **AGGRESSION IS HUMAN AND CAN EXIST IN ALL PLACES.**

- **AGGRESSION CAN BE INITIATED BY THE BELIEF IN HAVING MORE ABILITY THAN SOMEONE ELSE.**

- **THE MORE VIGOROUS TYPES ADAPT, EVOLVE MORE WITH NEW METHODS TO FACE NEW OR DIFFICULT CHALLENGES WHICH CAN MAKE THEM SUCCESSFUL.**

- **AGGRESSION CAN BE A BY-PRODUCT AND INCREASE OPPORTUNITIES IF SUPPORT IS AVAILABLE.**

- **TRIGGERS FOR AGRESSION MAY THOUGH NEED TO BE IDENTIFIED AND STAMPED ON IMMEDIATELY.**

- **INVASIVE ALIENS ARE OFTEN HOSTILE.**

- **SOME INVADERS HAVE DIFFERENT DEGREES OF TOXICITY AND THEIR EFFECTS CAN INCREASE THROUGH TIME OR BY CERTAIN ACTIONS.**

- **BE LIKE THE MOST AGGRESSIVE BRAMBLES WAVING YOUR SHOOTS, THRUSTING AHEAD RELENTLESSLY. CLIMB OVER ANYTHING IN THE WAY AND PROTECT YOURSELF WITH SPINES AS YOU DO THIS.**

13 DISPERSAL

'A good traveller is one who does not know where he is going to, and a perfect traveller does not know where he came from.'

The Importance of Living. Lin Yutang, (1938).

Weeds are experts at dispersal and can produce several generations in a single year. Businesses need to look at ways of spreading their influence and their products worldwide.

- **SMALL SEEDS OF BUSINESS TRAVEL THE BEST.**

- **ENERGY IS NEEDED TO PROPEL THE SPORES OF BUSINESS. SOMETIMES THIS IS EXPLOSIVE.**

- **SUPPORT LIKE PARACHUTES ARE NEEDED TO CARRY THE BUSINESS MESSAGE OR STRUCTURE HIGH INTO THE SKY FOR MILES.**

- **BIG BUSINESSES LIKE TREES AND CAN SPREAD THEIR INFLUENCE FURTHER.**

- **IN SPREADING BUSINESS SEEDS, LOTS MAY BE LOST BUT THIS IS OF NO CONSEQUENCE.**

- **OTHER EXTERNAL INFLUENCES OUT OF YOUR CONTROL MAY HELP RELEASE THE SEEDS.**

-

- **DON'T LOSE HOPE. SOME SEEDS TRAVEL FOR A LONG TIME BEFORE FINALLY BECOMING ESTABLISHED.**

- **ATTRACTIVE ILLUSIONS WILL HELP YOU GREATLY IN CARRYING SEEDS.**

- **NOTE SOME FRUITS OF BUSINESS MAY RIPEN AT DIFFERENT TIMES ATTRACTING DIFFERENT CUSTOMERS OR OPPORTUNITIES.**

- **OTHER BIG BUSINESSES MAY HELP YOU TRANSFER YOUR SEEDS.**

- **IF YOU HAVE ONLY A FEW EXPERIENCED STAFF OR EXPERIENCE IS TOO WIDE SPREAD THERE IS LESS CHANCE OF DISPERSAL AND MORE CHANCE OF COMPETITION FROM THOSE ALREADY ESTABLISHED.**

- **BUSINESSES MAY NEED SOME SORT OF HOOKS TO ATTACH AND BECOME SUCCESSFUL HITCHHIKERS.**

- **BUILD UP OF TENSION AND EXPENDITURE MAY HAVE AN EXPLOSIVE EFFECT.**

- **OPPORTUNISTS ARE USEFUL FOR NEW ORGANISATIONS TO CHANGE.**

- **QUALITY ENSURES THAT DISPERSAL WILL BE REWARDING.**

14 DORMANCY

*'We are ready for any
unforeseen event which may or
may not happen'*

**George W. Bush Jr,
(September 1995)**

For every business and plant there
is a time to waken. It just needs
the right stimulus to put things in
motion.

- **BUSINESSES, ESPECIALLY
  SEASONAL ONES, MAY
  SHUT DOWN AT TIMES OR
  PROGRESS SLOWER OR
  FASTER.**

- **RESOURCES MAY BE
  WITHDRAWN IN SOME
  CONDITIONS SO THAT
  ORGANISATIONS HAVE TO
  DEPEND ON WHAT HAS
  BEEN BUILT UP AND
  STORED.**

- IDENTIFY THOSE PEOPLE THAT REMAIN DORMANT MENTALLY AND PHYSIOLOGICALLY. THESE CAN STAND UP TO VIGOROUS CONDITIONS AND CAN COME OUT OF THE WORST CATASTROPHES UNSCATHED.

- SOME MAY REMAIN DORMANT AS THEIR EXPECTATIONS HAVE NOT YET BEEN MET.

- SOME MAY NEED SPECIAL PROJECTS OR THE RIGHT SITUATIONS, TIMES TO BREAK DORMANCY AND RESPOND.

- YOU NEED TO KNOW HOW STAFF REACT TO DIFFERENT SITUATIONS AND THEIR TOLERANCE OF DIFFERENT AMOUNTS OF STRESS.

- **SOME ORGANISATIONS HAVE DISTINCTIVE COMPOSITIONS OF STAFF AND STRUCTURES, ANY ADVANCES BEING KEPT DORMANT.**

- **PHYSICAL OR ENVIRONMENTAL CONDITIONS HAVE TO BE RIGHT TO BE READY TO BREAK DORMANCY.**

15 SUCCESSION

'I wandered lonely as a cloud

That floats on high oe'r vales and hills,

When all at once I saw a crowd,

A host of golden daffodils';

William Wordsworth, (1807)

A fertile organisation supports the growth of ideas as minor or large contributions for different groups so as to provide a mixture to carry on into the future.

- **YOU CAN FORM A PYRAMID BUSINESS BY PINCHING OUT THE TIP AND OUTSIDE SHOOTS.**

- **OPPORTUNITIES NOT AVAILABLE FOR ONE SECTION MAY COME BACK LATER TO BE BACK IN THE COMPETITION RACE. THESE CAN OVERTAKE THOSE WHO WERE EARLY SPRINTERS AND GREW TOO TALL TOO FAST.**

- **SOME ORGANISATIONS CAN THRIVE IN AREAS OF DISTURBANCE WITH OTHERS.**

- **CUTTING BACK CAN ENSURE THERE WILL BE A CUSHION FOR THE NEXT SEASON.**

- **SMALL FRAGMENTS OF IDEAS OR NEGATIVE AND POSITIVE IDEAS CAN WORK TOGETHER TO INFLUENCE THE WAY FORWARD.**

- YOU CAN ACCELERATE A SUPPLY CHAIN WHERE DEMAND CHANGES AND INCREASES ARE REQUIRED BY THE END USER.

- REDUCING WAITING TIMES CAN BE A TRADE OFF BETWEEN COST OF IMPROVED SERVICE TIME IS WASTED WHERE THE PERCIEVED WAITING TIME IS NOT ACTUAL WAITING TIME.

16 DYNAMIC PARTS

'Forgetting those things which are behind and reaching forth unto those things which are before.'

Bible (King James Version) Philippians 3:13

Larger essential sections of a business can have few problems and can survive many situations.

- **BEWARE OF GAPS IN AN ORGANISATION WHICH COMBINE TO AFFECT THE WHOLE ORGANISATION. DEAL WITH THEM IMMEDIATELY.**

- **YOU NEED TO KNOW THE SERIES OF SLOW CHANGES WHICH COULD CONTRIBUTE TO A LARGER DYNAMIC CHANGE.**

- **EXPANSION CAN OCCUR IN SMALL CREVICES WHERE A FOOTHOLD IS GAINED. THESE CAN INFLUENCE AND PENETRATE DEEP WITHIN THE FOUNDATIONS OF THE BUSINESS.**

- **SOME BUSINESSES CAN FEND FOR THEMSELVES WITHOUT CONSTANT ATTENTION BUT MAY TAKE YEARS TO FILL THE GAPS.**

- **CUT OUT DEAD WOOD AND ENSURE STAKING SUPPORT IS IN PLACE BEFORE FURTHER GROWTH.**

- **BEWARE OF POOR QUALITY GOODS THAT CAN DISAPPEAR AND REAPPEAR IN A NEW GUISE QUICKLY.**

- **THESE MAY BE HARD TO TRACE.**

- **USING SUPPORT CAN ALSO HELP COMPETITORS BRINGING THEM CLOSER TO SIMILAR AREAS OF WORK.**

- **PRODUCTION LINES ARRANGED WITH STAGES IN A U SHAPE WILL DETERMINE WORK IN ONE DIRECTION ONLY.**

- **YOU NEED FEEDBACK INFORMATION QUICKLY AT ALL LEVELS TO IMPROVE SUPPLY CHAINS AND QUALITY OF SERVICE RELATED TO DEMAND.**

17 TROUBLE SHOOTING

'Try to analyse situations intelligently, anticipate problems and move swiftly to solve them. However, when you are up to your ears in alligators, it is difficult to remember the reason you are there is to drain the swamp'.

Rumsfield (Donald) Rules. Serving in Government. (Source unknown) (Dec 1974).

There may be a gradual kind of weathering leading to gradual loss of mechanisms or ideas. This may depend on the extent of process time and the local climate. It is important to recognise the symptoms and troubles early on especially if structural.

- **GROWTH CAN BE MORE RESTRICTED IN A RESTRICTED ENVIRONMENT.**

- REPEATING THE SAME WORKING APPROACH FOR SEVERAL YEARS MAY NOT TAKE INTO ACCOUNT TRENDING AND SIDELINES.

- APPROPRIATENESS OF YOUR BUILDING MAY NO LONGER BE RIGHT. CHANGE WORKPLACE TO INTRODUCE FRESHNESS.

- WITH STRATIFICATION YOU NEED TO ENSURE LOWER LEVELS ARE MORE FERTILE AND CAN ACTUALLY PUT PROCESSES INTO PLACE.

- YOU CAN HAVE AREAS WHERE CHANGE IS HINDERED AND IDEAS ARE NOT FLOURISHING.

- STAFF ARE IMPERVIOUS AND ONLY SUPPORT SPECIFIC ROLES.

- **BEWARE OF STAGNATION AND LACK OF STIMULATION. ALTER WORK PATTERNS WITH OVERTIME AND EXTRA SHIFTS.**

- **PEOPLE LEAVING MAY RESULT IN A LOSS OF EXPERTISE AND IDEAS. THIS MUST BE BALANCED BY A TREND OF FLESHING OUT NEW IDEAS.**

- **CULTURE AND CLIMATE AFFECTS NATURE OF STAFF AND HASTENS OR SLOWS DOWN PROGRESS AND REPONSIVENESS.**

- **YOU CAN MINIMISE RESOURCES, PEOPLE AND EQUIPMENT BUT STILL MAINTAIN GOOD FLOW WHILE RESPECTING QUALITY AND CUSTOMER NEEDS.**

- BUILD IN TIME FOR EMERGENCIES.

- LOOK AT HOW TECHNOLOGY COULD HELP TURNOVER AND CUSTOMER NEEDS.

- DEFINE THE PROBLEM AND RUN EXPERIMENTS TO SIMULATE A NEW MODEL. THEN ANALYSE RESULTS.

- LOOK AT EFFECTS OF DECENTRALISING OR MAKING MORE WIDESPREAD SERVICES BUT ENHANCING CUSTOMER CONTACT.

- LOOK AT DOING WITHOUT A PRODUCT OR STAFF AND FIND WAYS OF MAKING YOUR SERVICE CHEAPER AND FASTER THAN COMPETITORS.

- **IDENTIFY CUSTOMERS PERCIEVED AND EXPECTED PERFORMANCE AND WHERE DISATISFACTION COULD BE EXPECTED.**

- **SERVICES CAN BE COPIED OR IMPROVED. NEED TO LOOK AT PACKAGING SO AS TO REDUCE COMPETITION.**

- **QUALITY COSTS AND FAILURE COSTS ALWAYS NEED TO BE ADDRESSED.**

- **ENSURE QUALITY GREATLY EXCEEDS EXPECTATIONS. MAKE IMPROVEMENTS AND MOVE ON.**

18 RIGHT CONDITIONS

'Success is a science; if you have the conditions, you get the result'

Oscar Wilde, (1883)

You may be the greatest show on earth, business or plant since the beginning of time but anyone can tell you that there is nothing seen without the right conditions

- **CHANGE ENVIRONMENTS WHERE POOR AND ALLOW PLENTY OF SPACE.**

- **ENSURE YOUR ENVIRONMENT SUPPORTS TALL GROWTH AND STABILITY ANCHORED AT BASE.**

- **WATCH OUT FOR BUILD UP OF PROBLEMS WHICH CAN CLOG UP CHANNELS OF FLOW IN YOUR BUSINESS.**

- **MAKE SURE YOUR ORGANISATION PROVIDES A PLATFORM IN WHICH A BUSINESS CAN GROW AND BE RECOGNISED. STEADY SUPPLIES ARE ESSENTIAL.**

19 CORRECT TIMING

'A good plan violently executed now is better than a perfect plan next week'

'War As I Knew It'. George S Patton. (1947).

Tolerance with even the smallest employee can extend into the roots of the organisation. This can only be seen by exposing the full role of the organisation. Need to understand how variations can affect activities.

- **RESCHEDULING IS DEPENDANT ON THE PLACE AND ROLE IN A SEQUENCE OF TASKS.**

- **ADJUSTMENTS CAN STILL MEAN AND OVERALL TIME MAY NOT CHANGE.**

- **YOU MUST BE FLEXIBLE AND USE TRIAL AND ERROR SO AS TO ELIMINATE WASTED TIME.**

- YOU MAY BE ABLE TO INTRODUCE AUTOMATION, BARCODES AND DATABASES.

- DON'T PAUSE BEFORE SORTING OUT PROBLEMS, SORT OUT STRAIGHT AWAY.

- DON'T PUT UP SPECIAL WALLS. TO SUCCEED DON'T WASTE TIME SEEKING APPROVAL FROM EVERYONE.

- MONITORING NEEDS TO BE ACCURATE AND UP TO DATE.

- HAVE HOTLISTS WHERE JOBS NEED TO BE DONE QUICKLY WITH DEADLINES.

- WORK OUT JOB RATES AND HOW LONG EQUIPMENT STAYS IDLE.

- USE SPECIALIST TIMETABLES TO LOOK AT SESSION AND CYCLE TIMES.

- SEE WHERE STAFF CAN HELP OTHER STAFF.

- WORK OUT CRITICAL PATHS, BEING LONGEST PATHS OF ACTIVITIES FROM START TO FINISH AND ADJUST.

- COMPARE INPUT WITH OUTPUT AND WORK OUT BACKLOG TO ENSURE IT STAYS MANAGEABLE IT IS DIFFICULT TO RECTIFY AND CONTROL LATER.

- FEASIBLE VERSUS DESIRABLE SCHEDULING NEEDS TO BE USED FOR FORECASTING TO HELP STOP BOTTLENECKS.

- **TRADE OFF BETWEEN TIME AND COST.**

- **LOOK AT COSTS TO REDUCE TIME OF AN ACTIVITY.**

- **SHORT OR MEDIUM FORECASTS CAN BE MADE BUT PAST DATA PREDICTIONS MAY NOT BE TOTALLY ACCURATE AS CIRCUMSTANCES CHANGE.**

- **FORECASTS NEED TO BE CONTINUALLY REVIEWED SO AS TO GIVE THE COMPETITIVE EDGE.**

20 RIGHT MIX

'Surround yourself with the best people you can find, delegate authority, and don't interfere'

Ronald Reagan, Interview with Fortune Magazine (September 1986).

In every office there is a different make up of individuals in a team. Some characteristics are common to particular types of organisations with a common composition and structure

- **CHANCE PLAYS A PART IN INITIAL STAFF SELECTION BUT SELECTION AND ROLE IS TIGHTENED AS AN ORGANISATION GROWS.**

- YOU NEED TO PRUNE
  PROPERLY TO SHAPE THE
  ORGANISATION AND GET
  REGULAR PRODUCTION.

- SOME NEW MEMBERS
  WILL THRIVE WHILE FOR
  OTHERS CONDITIONS MAY
  BE UNFAVOURABLE AND
  THEY MAY LEAVE.

- SURVIVAL DEPENDS ON
  THE ABILITY TO
  TOLERATE THE
  CONDITIONS IN THE
  HABITAT BUT THESE
  COULD STILL CHANGE.

- MAJOR PLAYERS GIVE THE
  BUSINESS A DEFINITE
  STRUCTURE WHICH IS
  IMPORTANT WHEN
  REMOVING STAFF OR
  CHANGING ROLES.

- **YOU NEED TO BE AWARE THAT INTERACTIONS BETWEEN STAFF ARE IMPORTANT. SOME MAY FORM GROUPS.**

- **ADJACENT STAFF CAN AFFECT PERFORMANCE AND CHANGES MAY NEED TO BE MADE.**

- **STAFF CAN BE TRAINED IN MORE THAN ONE JOB ROLE SO THAT COVER CAN BE FOUND FOR STAFF ABSENCES.**

21 FAILURE AND MISTAKES

'Mistakes are a fact of life. It is the response to error that counts'

'Of Liberation'. Nikki Giovanni (1970).

As with plants there can be mistakes, the final product not being what one expected. Progress was never made without mistakes, the human race can tell you that.

- **TOO MUCH EMPHASIS ON PRODUCTION METHODS AND NOT ON FINAL PRODUCT CAN CAUSE PROBLEMS.**

- **IMPATIENCE CAN LEAD TO MISTAKES AND OVERPRODUCTION CAN HAVE KNOCK ON EFFECTS.**

- **YOU MAY NEED ANNUAL CUTBACKS TO HELP IMPROVE YIELD AND QUALITY.**

- **POOR LOCATION MAY INHIBIT GROWTH PUTTING STRESS ON THE ORGANISATION.**

- **NEED TO LEARN FROM MISTAKES AND ALLOW THE CURRENT CLIMATE TO GUIDE YOU.**

- **TO CUSTOMERS LACK OF FAIRNESS, LACK OF COMFORT, INCREASED ANXIOUS WAITS AS WELL AS POOR PREVIOUS EXPERIENCES CAN RESULT IN LOSS OF BUSINESS.**

- **CHOOSING LOW PRICES FOR PRODUCTS MAY SUGGEST TO CUSTOMERS THAT WHATS IN THE PACKET MAY NOT BE WHAT THEY HAVE PAID FOR.**

- **LATENESS OR WRONG INFORMATION WILL ALWAYS HAVE A NEGATIVE EFFECT. IT IS VITAL THAT THE PRODUCER COMMUNICATES WITH THE CUSTOMER.**

22 ADAPTATION

'Natural enemies may provide significant selection for the relevant morphologies'

Bernays et al. Philosophical Transactions (August. 1991).

It is suggested that natural enemies may provide significant selection for the relevant morphologies. Extra numbers of businesses or organisations are built up over many years through the activities of people themselves. These are influenced by the political and social climate. Where the economic climate is harsh then the balance may be affected and the overall productivity changed.

- **NON RAPID DETERIORATION ALLOWS BUSINESSES TO USE THEIR EXPERIENCE TO HELP CONTINUE WITH SUCCESS.**

- **IF DETERIORATION OCCURS ON A LARGE SCALE AND DIFFERS FROM PAST EXPERIENCE TECHNOLOGICAL ADVANCES CAN TAKE OVER.**

- **YOU MAY HAVE TO REMOVE BUSINESS ROOTS AND REPLANT ELSEWHERE AS YOU ARE ESTABLISHED IN WRONG PLACE.**

- **CHANGES CAN ALLOW BETTER USE OF FACILITIES THAN BEFORE AND LEAD TO GREATER SUCCESS.**

23 ADVERTISING

'Many a small thing has been made large by the right kind of advertising'

From 'A Connecticut Yankee in King Arthurs Court'. Mark Twain (1889)

- **ADVERTS NEED TO BE A GIANT HAZE OF COLOUR THAT WEAVES A STORY OR SLOGAN.**

- **ADVERTS CAN CREATE A SENSE OF ENTRANCE TOWARDS A PRODUCT OR SERVICE.**

- **THE ADVERT'S MESSAGE MAY NOT BLOW IN THE RIGHT DIRECTION OR MAY REACH THE WRONG. CUSTOMERS SO SEVERAL DIFFERENT FORMS OF ADVERTISING ARE ESSENTIAL.**

- **ADVERTS NEED TO PORTRAY A CENTRE OF EXCELLENCE WITH REFERENCE TO PAST POSITIVE. FEEDBACK FROM SATISFIED PARTNERS, STAFF OR SERVICE USERS.**

- **ADVERTS CAN REACH THE MARKET AT A PREMIUM PRICE WHICH RESPONDS TO OTHER COMPETITORS. THIS CAN BE ESPECIALLY EFFECTIVE AS THE ANNOUNCEMENT OF INTRODUCTION OF A NEW PRODUCT OR SERVICE.**

ABOUT THE AUTHOR

Dr Mike Pearce is a biologist interested in behavior. He is a scientist who has worked in this country and overseas. Previously he was a manager of a Health and Social Care section at a college in Canterbury, Kent. There is a link between living things and ideas in business. Plant success forms an ideal subject for comparison and weeds especially, like a business, can last forever.